GIGGLY
RHYMES

For Rachel and Richard

GIGGLY RHYMES

Selected and
illustrated by
Julie Park

LITTLE
MAMMOTH

Auntie Agnes's Cat

My Auntie Agnes has a cat.
I do not like to tell her that
Its body seems a little large
(With lots of stripes for camouflage)
Its teeth and claws are also larger
Than they ought to be. A rajah
Gave her the kitten, I recall,
When she was stationed in Bengal.
But that was many years ago,
And kittens are inclined to grow.
So now she has a fearsome cat –
But I don't like to tell her that.

Colin West

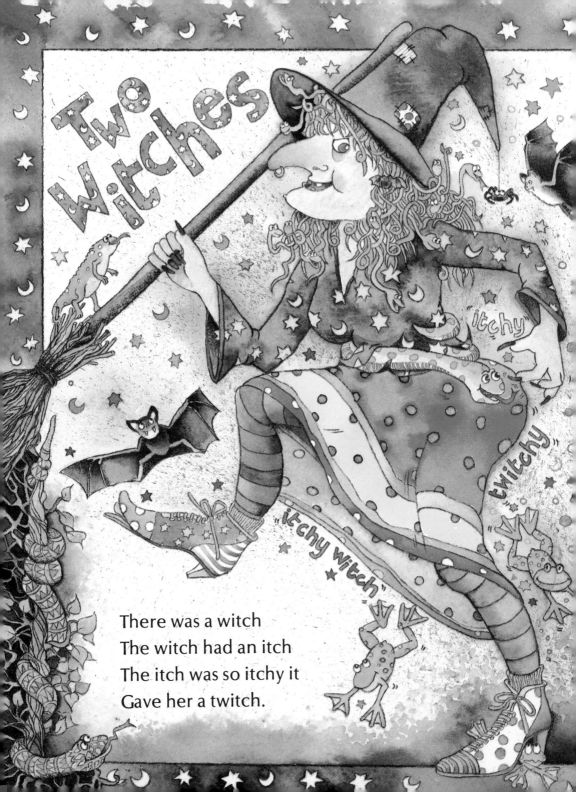

Two Witches

There was a witch
The witch had an itch
The itch was so itchy it
Gave her a twitch.

Another witch
Admired the twitch
So she started twitching
Though she had no itch.

Now both of them twitch
So it's hard to tell which
Witch has the itch and
Which witch has the twitch.

Alexander Resnikoff

Baboon

There was a Baboon
Who, one afternoon,
Said, 'I think I will fly to the sun,'
So, with two great palms
Strapped to his arms,
He started his take-off run.

Mile after mile
He galloped in style
But never once left the ground,
'You're running too slow,'
Said a passing crow,
'Try reaching the speed of sound.'

So, he put on a spurt –
By God how it hurt!
The soles of his feet caught fire
There were great clouds of steam
As he raced through a stream
But he still didn't get any higher.

Racing on through the night,
Both his knees caught alight
And smoke billowed out from his rear.
Quick to his aid
Came a fire brigade
Who chased him for over a year.

Many moons passed by,
Did Baboon ever fly?
Did he ever get to the sun?
I've just heard today
That he's well on his way!
He'll be passing through Acton at one.

P.S. Well, what do you expect from a Baboon?

Spike Milligan

Behold the wonders of the mighty deep,
Where crabs and lobsters learn to creep,
And little fishes learn to swim,
And clumsy sailors tumble in.

ANON

EGGS

All kinds of creatures come from eggs –
Canaries, owls and larks,
And turtles, insects, crocodiles,
And fish and snakes and sharks –
When next at breakfast you should have
Boiled eggs, why then look out!
In opening them be sure that one
Of these does not hop out.

Cecil G. Trew

He has opened all his parcels
    but the largest and the last;
His hopes are at their highest
    and his heart is beating fast;
O Happy Hippopotamus,
    what lovely gift is here?
He cuts the string. The world stands still
    A pair of boots appear!

The Hippo's Birthday

O Little Hippopotamus,
    the sorrows of the small!
He dropped two tears to mingle
    with the flowing Senegal;
And the 'Thank you' that he uttered
    was the saddest ever heard
In the Senegambian jungle
    from the mouth of beast or bird.

E.V. RiEU.

Through every nook and every cranny
The wind blew in on poor old Granny;
Around her knees, into each ear
(And up her nose as well, I fear).

All through the night the wind grew
                                    worse,
It nearly made the vicar curse.
The top had fallen off the steeple
Just missing him (and other people).

It blew on man; it blew on beast.
It blew on nun; it blew on priest.
It blew the wig off Auntie Fanny –
But most of all, it blew on Granny!

The Owl and the Pussy-Cat went to sea
   In a beautiful pea-green boat:
They took some honey, and plenty of money
   Wrapped up in a five-pound note.
The Owl looked up to the stars above,
   And sang to a small guitar,
'O lovely Pussy, O Pussy, my love,
   What a beautiful pussy you are,
         You are,
         You are!
   What a beautiful Pussy you are!'

Pussy said to the owl, 'You elegant fowl,
   How charmingly sweet you sing!
Oh! let us be married; too long we have tarried
   But what shall we do for a ring?'
They sailed away, for a year and a day,
   To the land where the bong-tree grows;
And there in a wood a Piggy-wig stood,
   With a ring at the end of his nose,
         His nose,
         His nose,
   With a ring at the end of his nose.

      'Dear pig, are you willing to sell for one shilling
        Your ring?' Said the piggy, 'I will.'
     So they took it away, and were married next day
       By the turkey who lives on the hill.
     They dined on mince and slices of quince,
       Which they ate with a runcible spoon;
     And hand in hand, on the edge of the sand,
       They danced by the light of the moon.

Edward Lear

I eat my peas with honey,
I have done all my life,
They do taste kind of funny
But it keeps them on the knife.

Appreciation

Auntie, did you feel no pain
Falling from that willow tree?
Will you do it, please, again?
'Cos my friend here didn't see.

Harry Graham

The Underwater Camel

The underwater Camel
Lives in streams and lakes and pools,
His hobbies are collecting stamps
And jumping over stools,

He likes to wear pyjamas
And play the slide trombone,
And if you ring his number
He'll play it down the 'phone.

Jonathan Allen

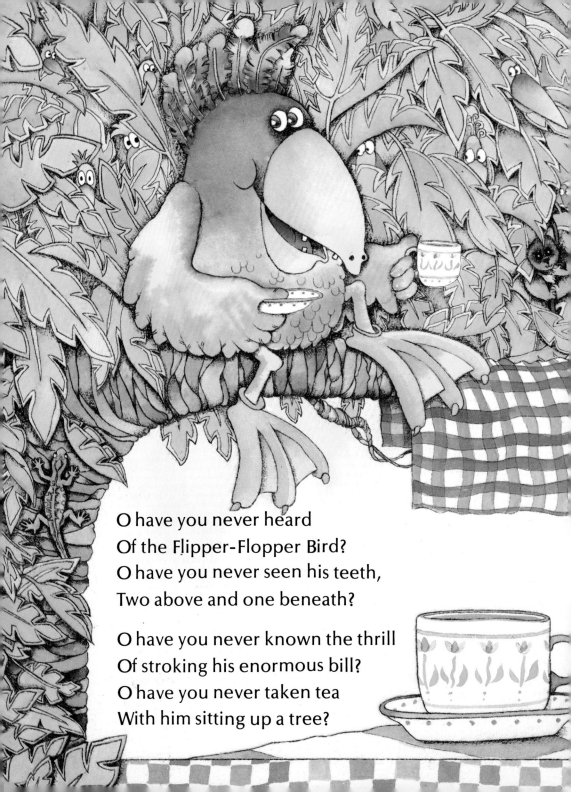

O have you never heard
Of the Flipper-Flopper Bird?
O have you never seen his teeth,
Two above and one beneath?

O have you never known the thrill
Of stroking his enormous bill?
O have you never taken tea
With him sitting up a tree?

Flipper Flopper Bird

O have you never seen him hop
As he goes a-flip a-flop?
O have you never heard his cry?
No, you've never? Nor have I.

Colin West

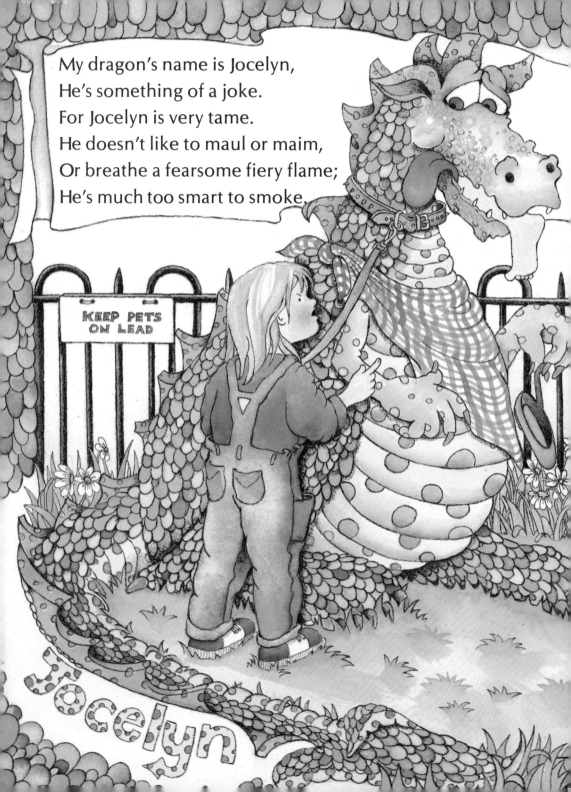

My dragon's name is Jocelyn,
He's something of a joke.
For Jocelyn is very tame.
He doesn't like to maul or maim,
Or breathe a fearsome fiery flame;
He's much too smart to smoke.

KEEP PETS
ON LEAD

Jocelyn

And when I take him to the park
The children form a queue,
And say, 'What lovely eyes of red!'
As one by one they pat his head.
And Jocelyn is so well-bred,
He only eats a few!

Colin West

CATS

Meeow Purr Meeow

sleepy cat snoring in a stripy chair

lazy cat lounging on a little window-ledge

dozy cat dreaming in a messy drawer

Daring cat dreaming in a dark dogs kennel

BUTCH

silly cat snoozing in a smelly sneaker

Cats sleep
   Anywhere
   Any table,
   Any chair

Top of piano,
Window-ledge,
In the middle,
On the edge,

Open drawer,
Empty shoe,
Anybody's lap
Will do

Fitted in a
   Cardboard box,
   In the cupboard
   With your frocks,

Anywhere.
They don't care
Cats sleep
Anywhere.

Eleanor Farjeon

Meeow Purr

Said a tiny Ant
To the Elephant,
'Mind how you tread in this clearing!'
But alas! cruel fate!
She was crushed by the weight
Of an elephant, hard of hearing.

When people call this beast to mind
They marvel more and more
    At such a little tail behind
So large a trunk before.

Auntie Agnes's Cat, The Flipper Flopper Bird,
and *Jocelyn, My Dragon* by Colin West from
"Not to be taken seriously" reprinted by permission
of Hutchinson, an imprint of Century Hutchinson

Two Witches from "Oh, How Silly" by Alexander Resnikoff.
Copyright © 1970. Reprinted by permission of
Mrs Joan Resnikoff

Silly Old Baboon and *Ant and Elephant* by Spike Milligan
from "A Book of Milliganimals" and *Granny*
by Spike Milligan from "Silly Verse for Kids"
reprinted by permission of Spike Milligan Productions Ltd

The Hippopotamus's Birthday by E V Rieu from
"The Flattered Flying Fish" reprinted by permission of Methuen

Appreciation by Harry Graham from "Ruthless Rhymes"
reprinted by permission of Edward Arnold Publishers Ltd

The Underwater Camel by Jonathan Allen from
"A Bad Case of Animal Nonsense" reprinted by
permission of J M Dent & Sons Ltd

Cats by Eleanor Farjeon from "The Children Bells'
reprinted by permission of Oxford University Press

Thank You

First published in Great Britain in 1988
by Methuen Children's Books

Published 1989 by Little Mammoth
an imprint of Mandarin Paperbacks
Michelin House, 81 Fulham Road, London SW3 6RB
Mandarin is an imprint of the Octopus Publishing Group

Reprinted 1991

Illustrations copyright © 1988 Julie Park
ISBN 0 7497 0217 6
Printed in Great Britain by Scotprint Ltd., Musselburgh.

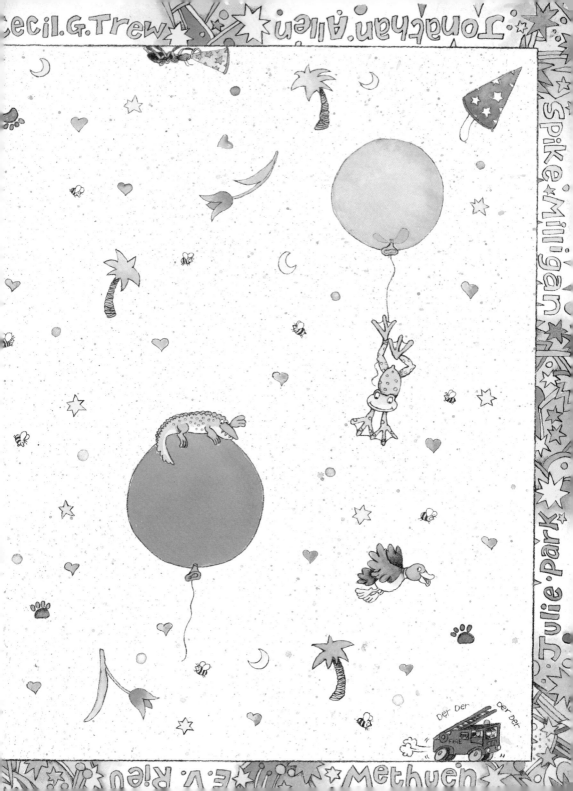